How to Draw

Food

For Jesse, Jasmine, Justin, Jordan, Melina, and Matthew

Published in the United States of America by The Child's World®
1980 Lookout Drive • Mankato, MN 56003-1705
800-599-READ • www.childsworld.com

Acknowledgments
Illustration and Design: Rob Court
Production: The Creative Spark, San Juan Capistrano, CA

Library of Congress Cataloging-in-Publication Data
Court, Rob, 1956–
How to draw food / by Rob Court.
p. cm. — (Doodle books)
ISBN 978-1-59296-953-1 (library bound : alk. paper)
1. Food in art—Juvenile literature. 2. Drawing—Technique—Juvenile literature. I. Title. II. Series.

NC825.F66C68 2008
743'.896413—dc22

2007013388

The Scribbles Institute™

Doodle Books™

How to Draw Food

by Rob Court

The Child's World®

muffin

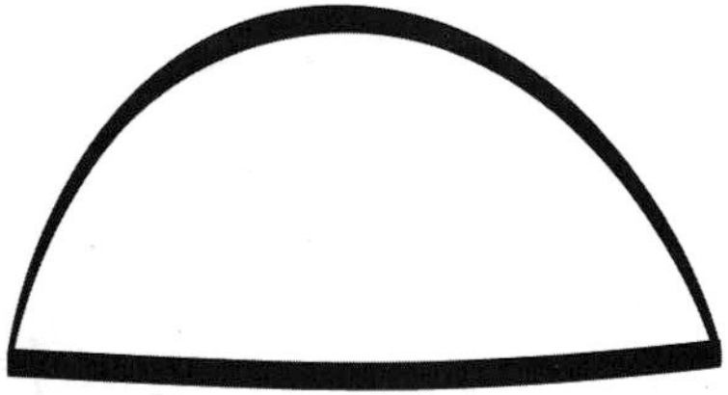

1

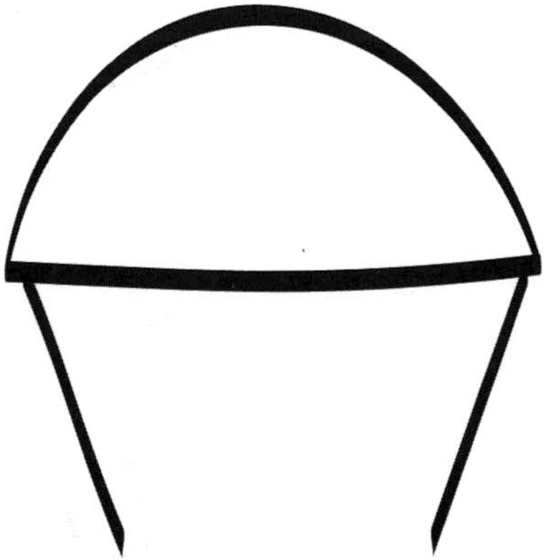

2

3

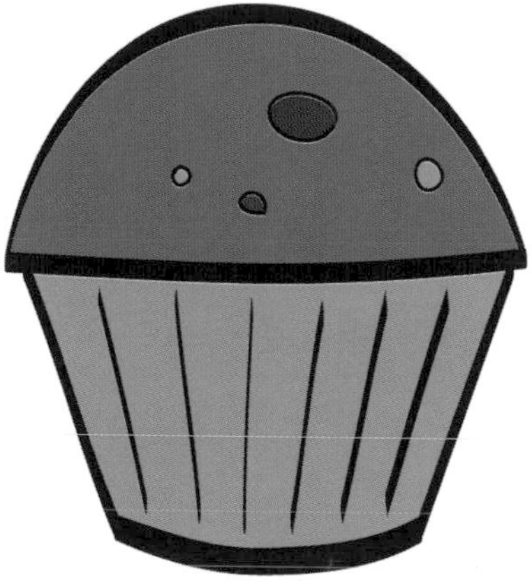

4

grapes

1

2

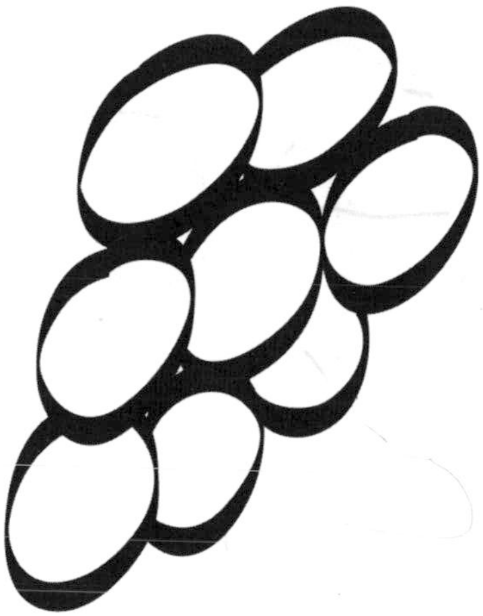

3

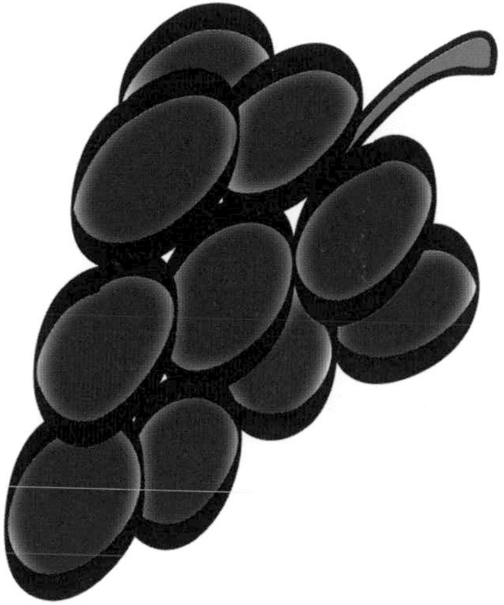

4

cookies

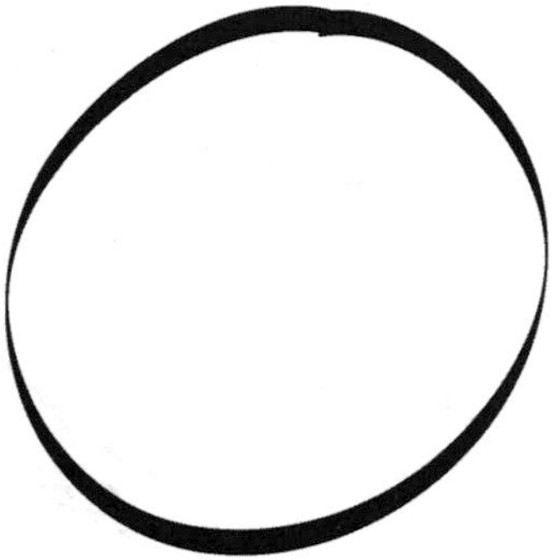

1

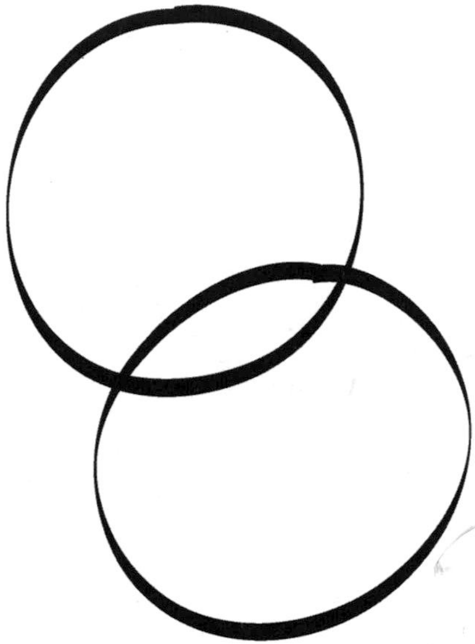

2

3

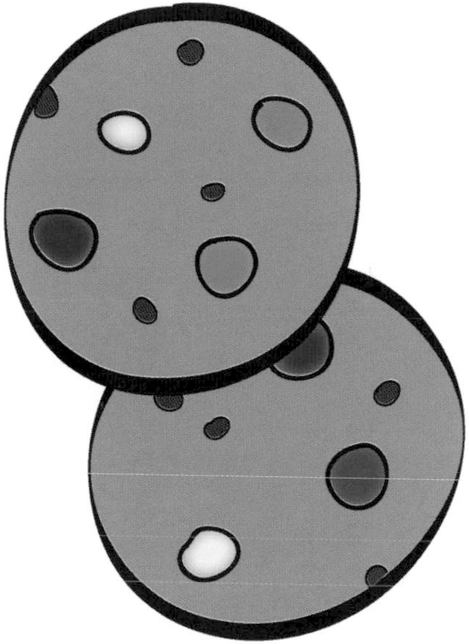

4

apple

1

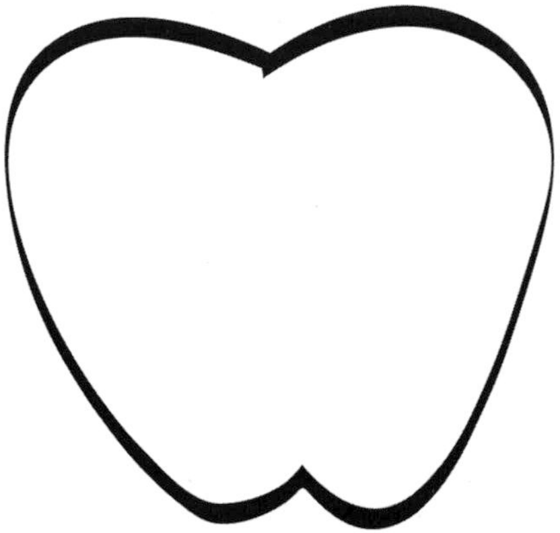

2

3

4

pizza

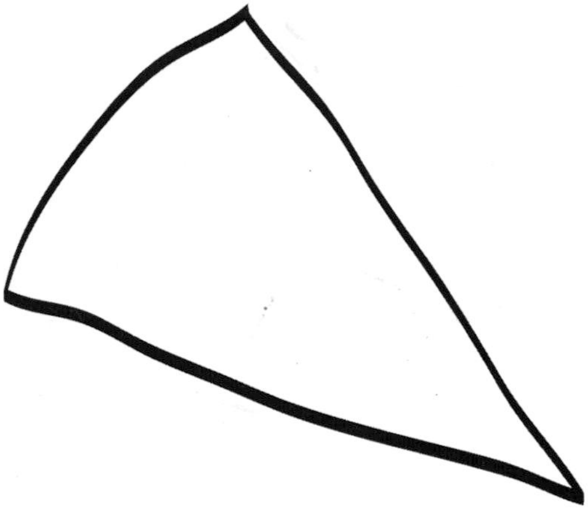

1

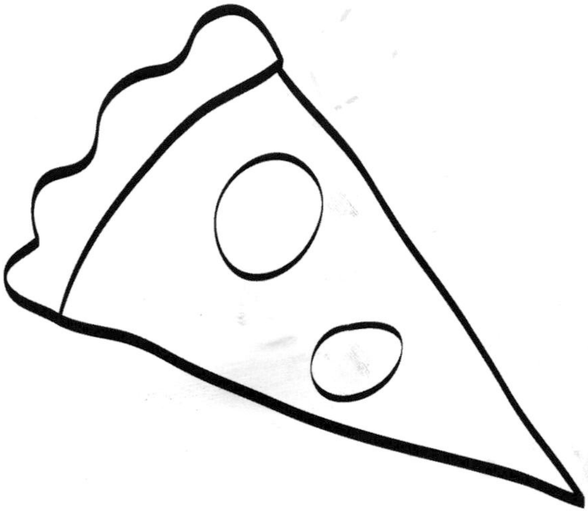

2

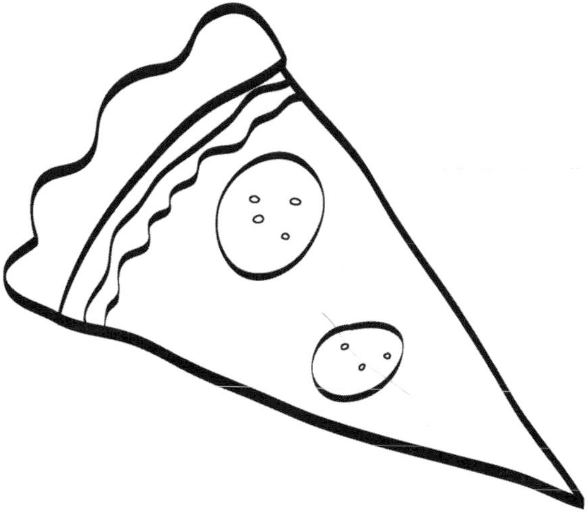

3

4

egg

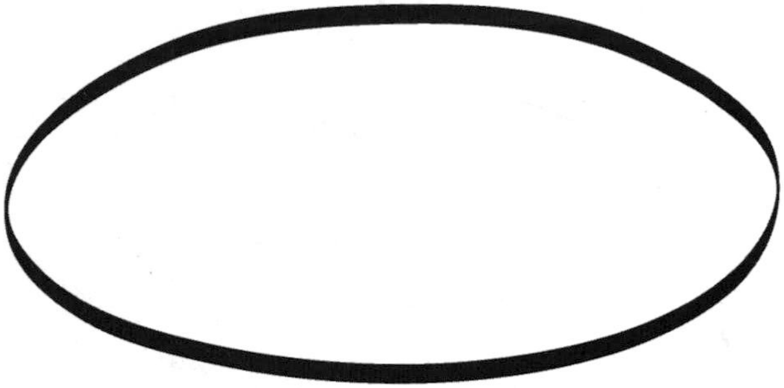

1

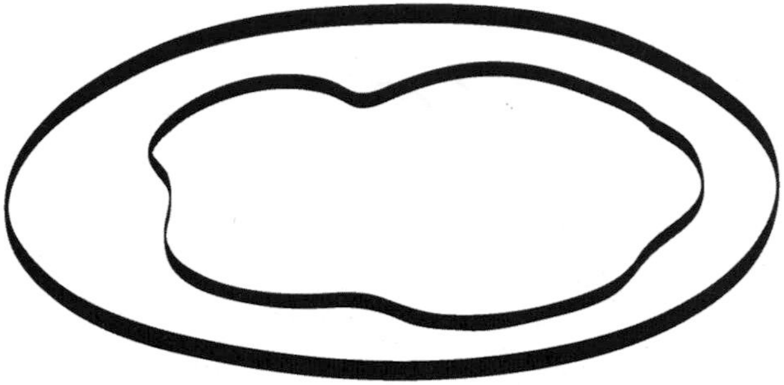

2

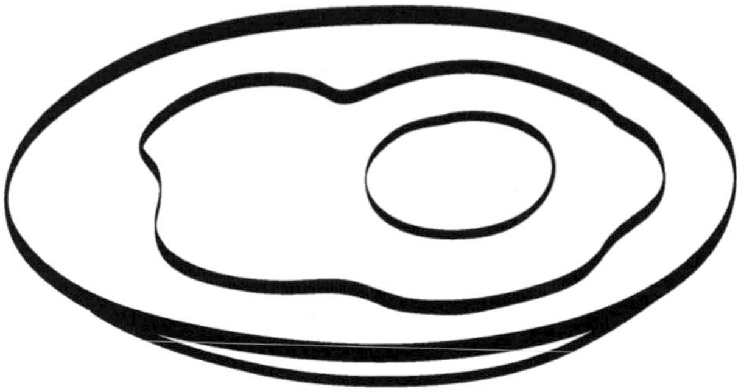

3

4

taco

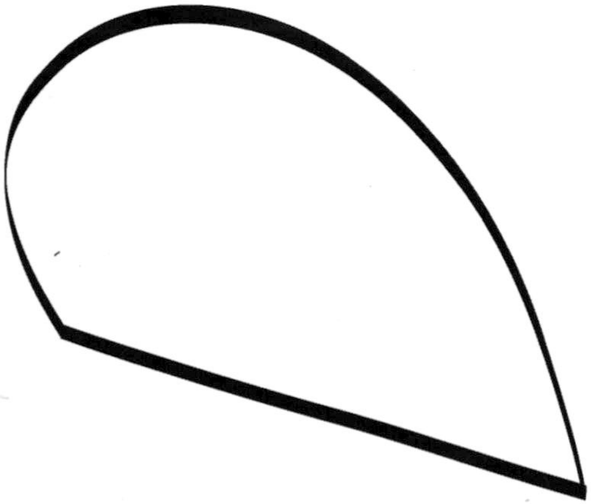

1

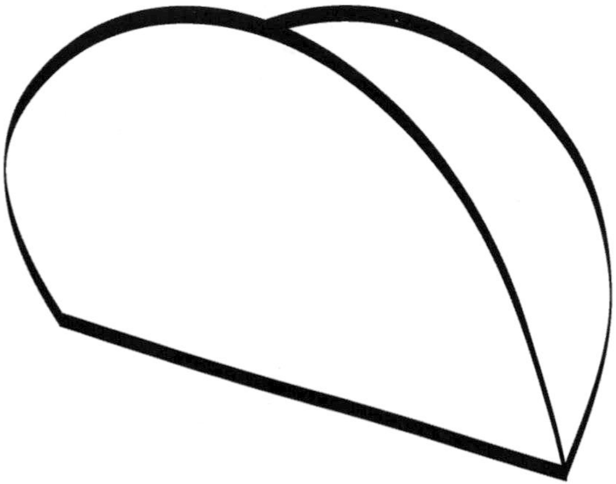

2

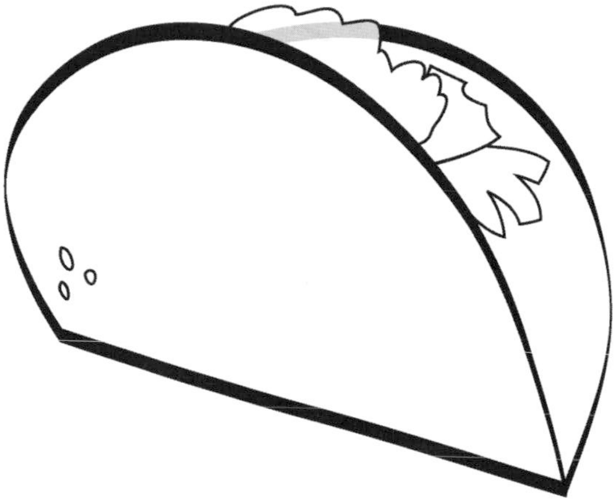

3

4

carrot

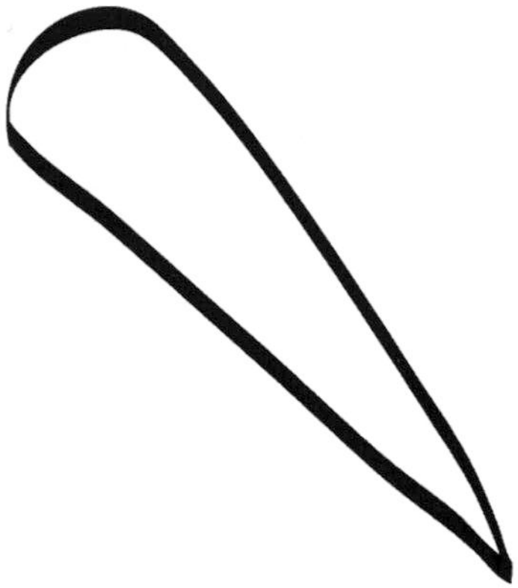

1

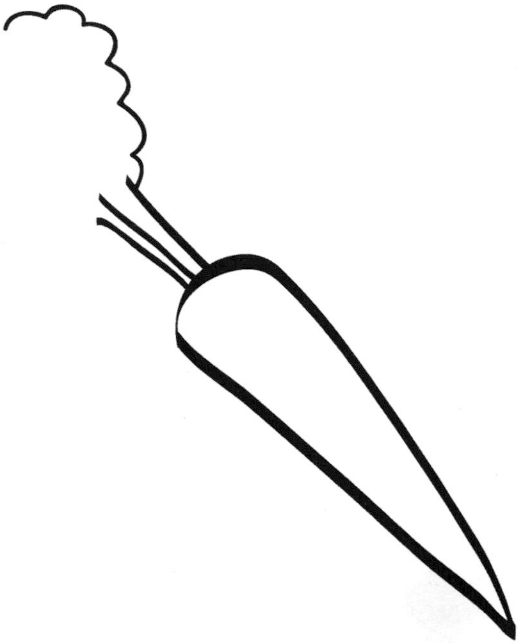

2

3

4

ice cream

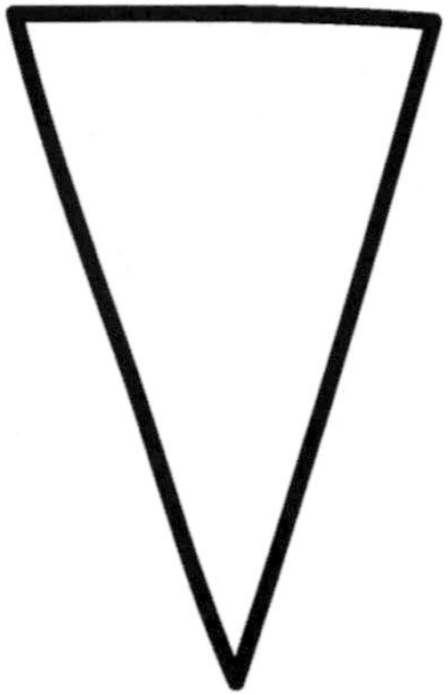

1

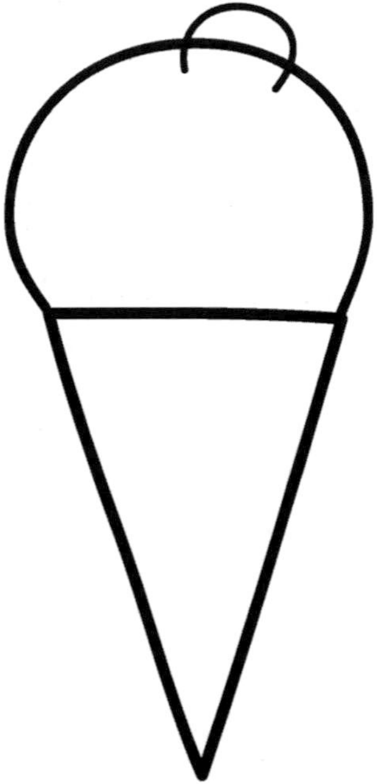

2

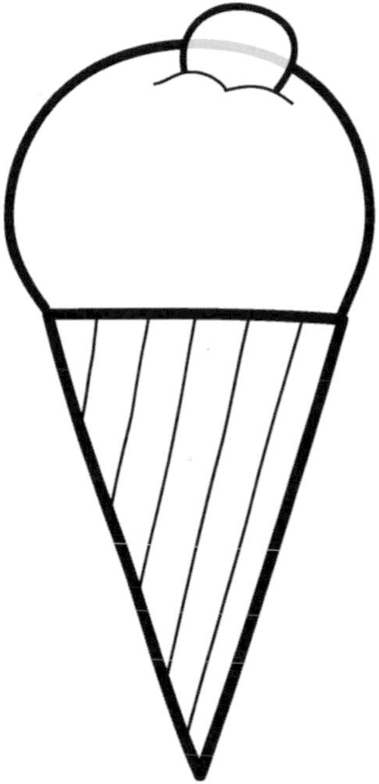

3

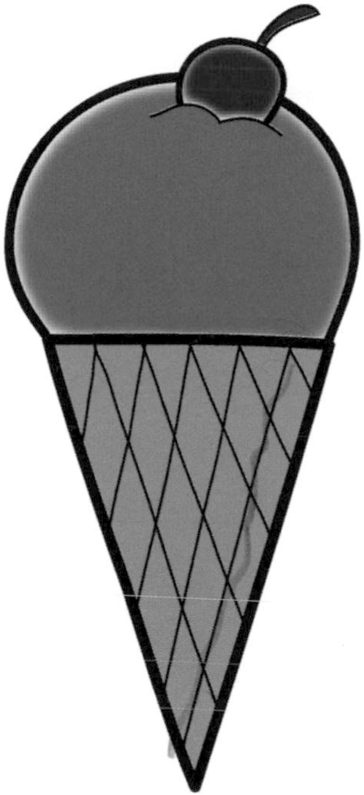

4

hot dog

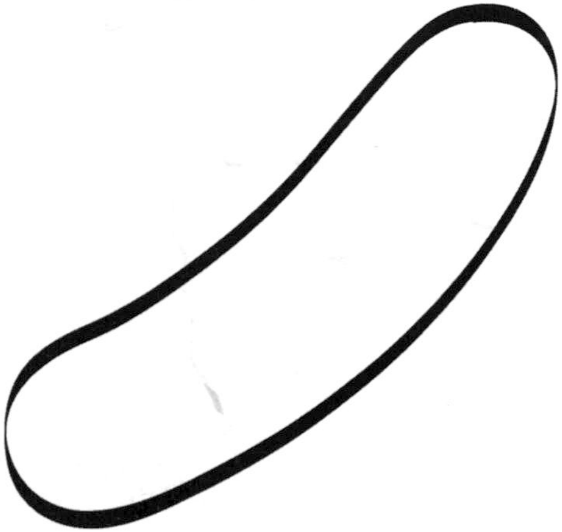

1

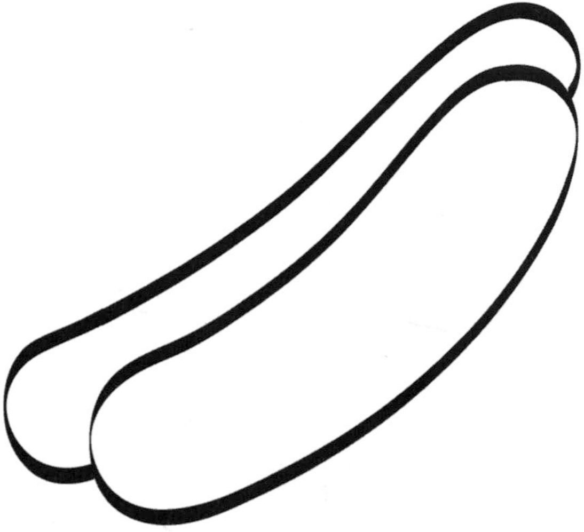

2

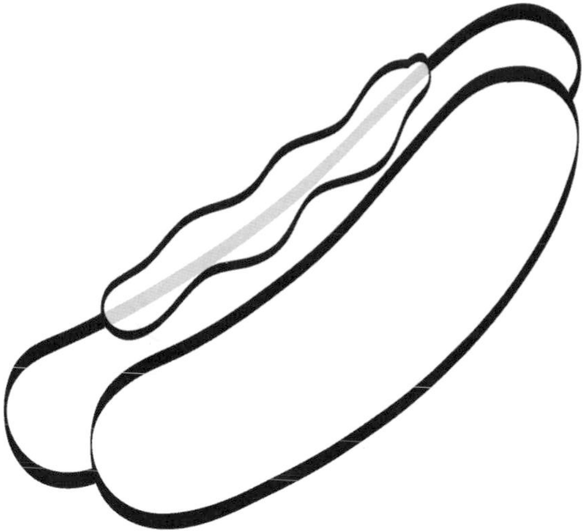

3

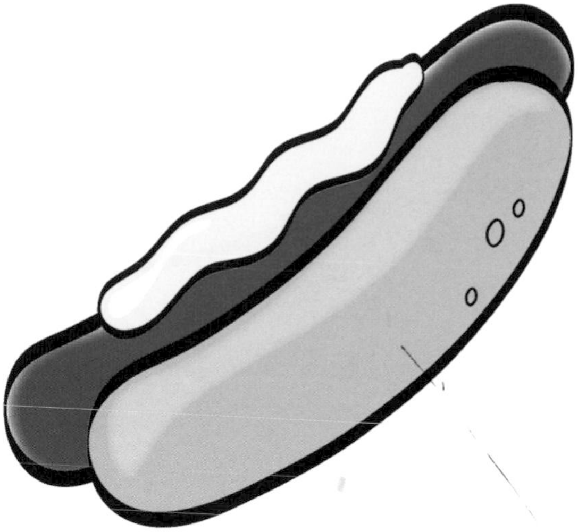

4

cake

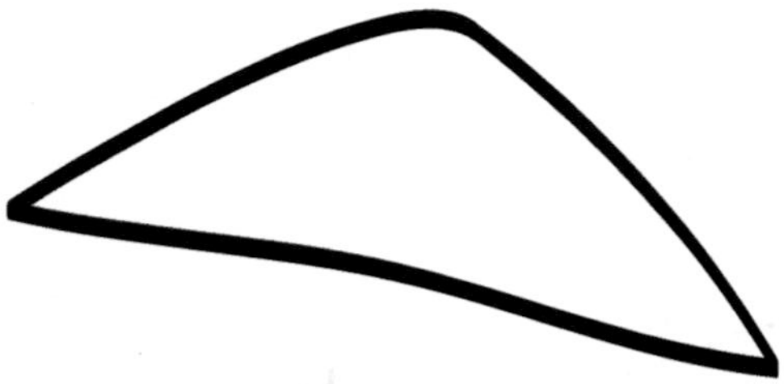

1

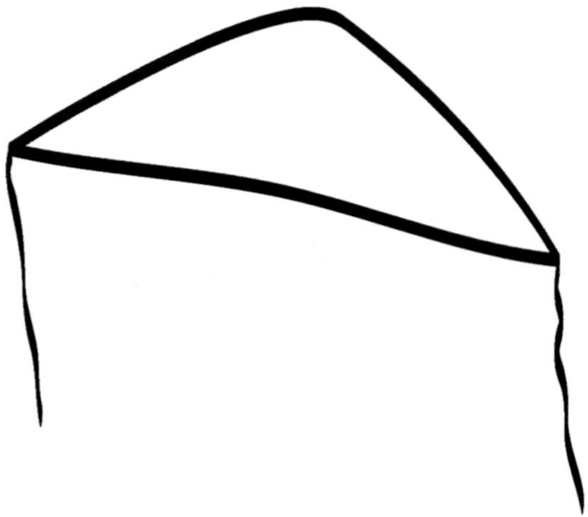

2

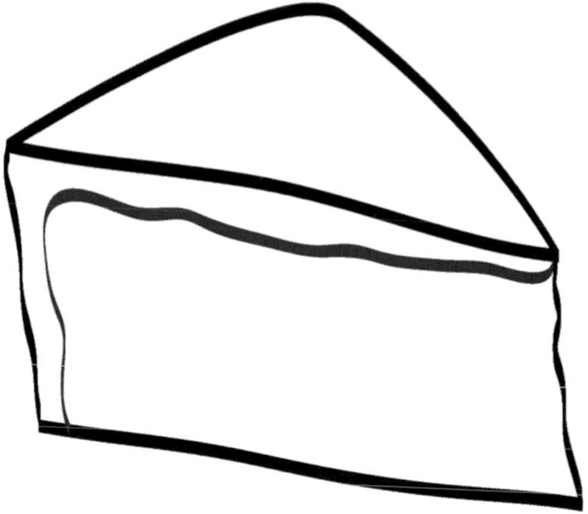

3

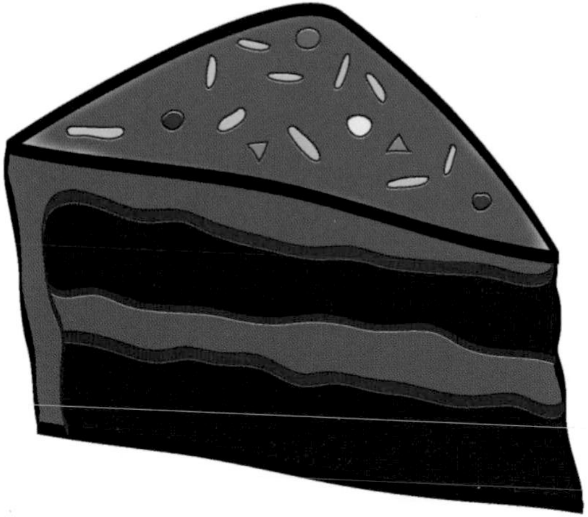

4

cheeseburger

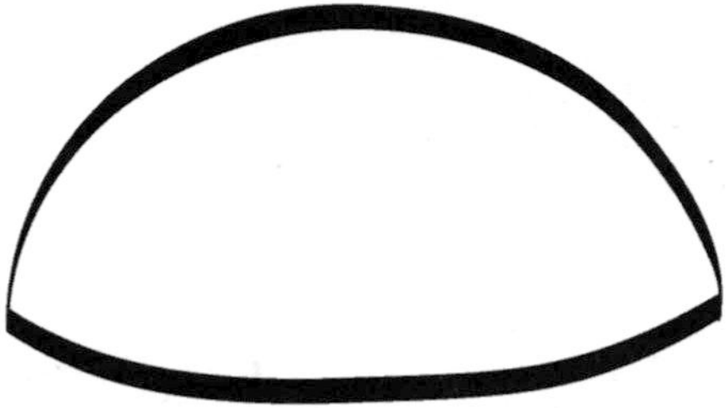

1

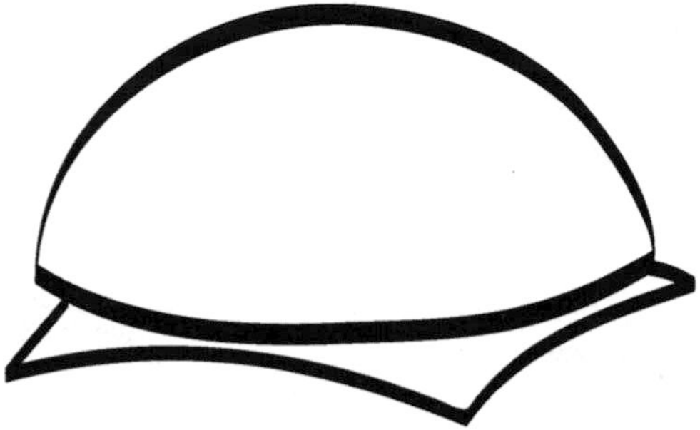

2

3

4

pie

1

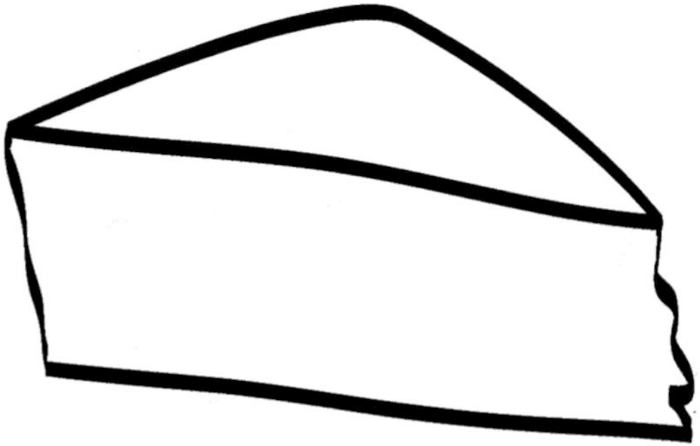

2

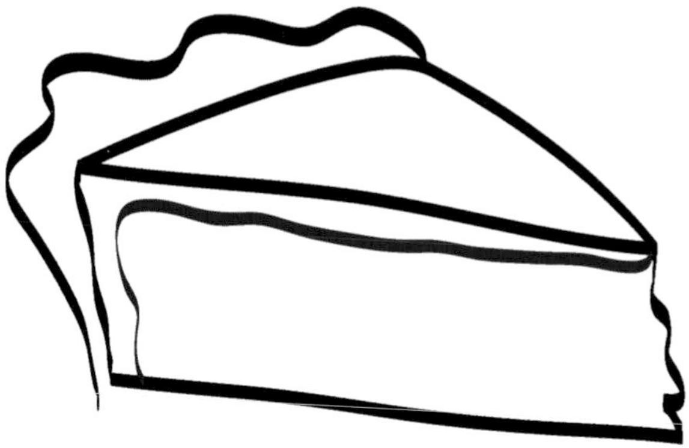

3

4

corn

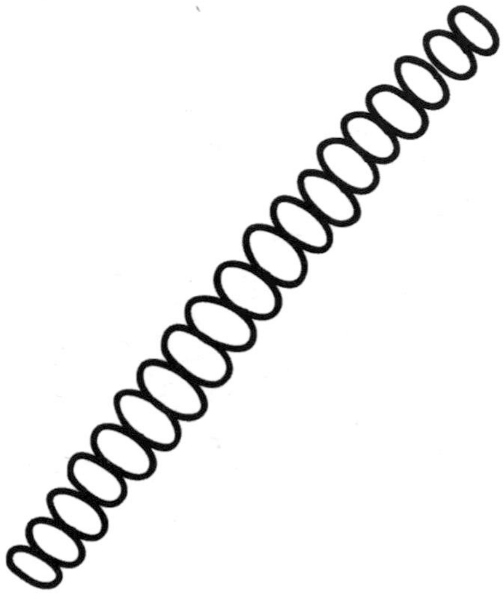

1

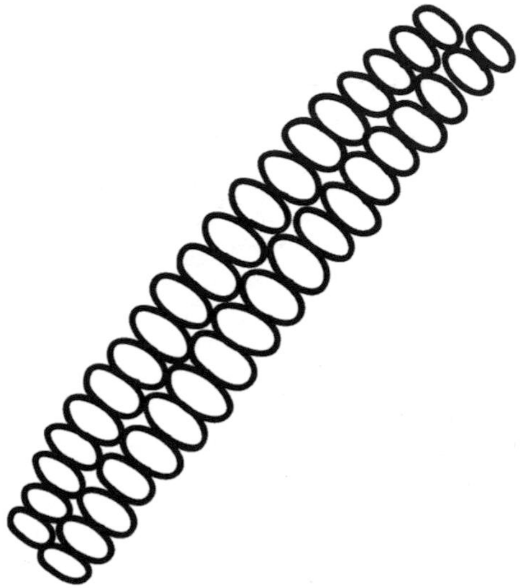

2

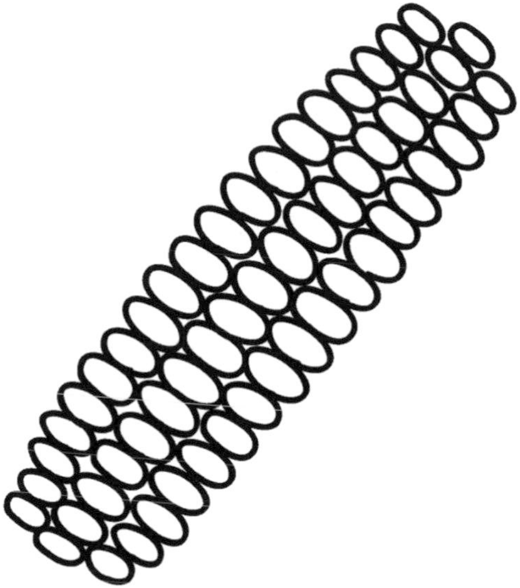

3

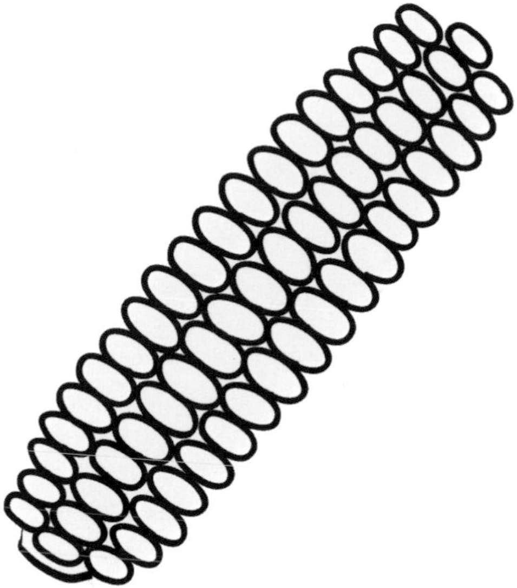

4

lines

horizontal

vertical

angled

curved

thick

thin

dotted

squiggly

dashed

point

loop

Move a point to make a line.

Connect lines to make a shape.

Shapes make all kinds of wonderful things!

Repeating dots, lines, and shapes makes patterns.

About the Author

Rob Court is a graphic artist and illustrator. He started the Scribbles Institute to help students, parents, and teachers learn about drawing and visual art. Please visit www.scribblesinstitute.com